A TI⌐
THERE WAS

Toni

East Preston in the early 1900s

A TIME
THERE WAS

*Memories of Rural Life
in Sussex*

PHŒBE SOMERS

WEALD & DOWNLAND OPEN AIR MUSEUM

ALAN SUTTON

First published in the United Kingdom in 1993
Alan Sutton Publishing Ltd · Phoenix Mill · Stroud · Gloucestershire
in association with
Weald and Downland Open Air Museum · Singleton · Chichester · Sussex

---

First published in the United States of America in 1993
Alan Sutton Publishing Inc. · 83 Washington Street · Dover · NH 03820

Reprinted 1994

British Library Cataloguing in Publication Data

Somers, Phœbe
   Time There Was: Memories of Rural Life in Sussex
   I. Title
   942.25082

   ISBN 0-7509-0385-6

Library of Congress Cataloging in Publication Data

Somers, Phœbe.
   A time there was : memories of rural life in Sussex /
      p. cm.
   ISBN 0-7509-0385-6 : £6.99
   1. West Sussex (England)–Social life and customs.   2. Somers,
   Phœbe–Homes and haunts–England–West Sussex.   3. Country life–
   England–West Sussex.   I. Title.
   DA670.W496S66   1993
   942.2'6082–dc20
                                                         93–26282
                                                              CIP

Typeset in 12/13 Sabon.
Typesetting and origination by
Alan Sutton Publishing Limited.
Printed in Great Britain by
The Bath Press, Avon.

Contents

List of Photographs

Foreword by Her Grace, Lavinia, Duchess of Norfolk

This amusing and informative book about old Sussex people is full of anecdotes, much of it captured in their own words and phrases.

It gives fascinating details of their childhood, their homes, schools and early working days, and is a picture of rustic life at the turn of the century.

Phœbe Somers interviewed more than five hundred people for her weekly articles which appeared regularly in the *West Sussex Gazette* for fourteen years. From these she has made a selection which she has rewritten and collated, giving detailed accounts of country life in Sussex between the 1890s and 1930s.

A Time There Was will make a most acceptable addition to any collection of books on Sussex.

Lavinia Norfolk.

Preface

For some fourteen years I talked with more than five hundred old country people in and around the vicinity of the hamlet of Poling, in West Sussex.

We talked about their early days, their families, their childhood, schools, work, village life, pleasures and hardships and life on the farms. The all-important work done by the women and girls in domestic service proved to be most revealing. These old people were not only amazingly articulate; they had vivid memories of their early life and they enjoyed recalling days which have now gone for ever.

I have brought together within these pages some of their personal memories, revealing little pockets of the old life, using, where possible, their own words and phrases.

Acknowledgements

I am most grateful to the many people whom I have interviewed and have featured in this book.

I am particularly grateful to Mr John Kendall, the former editor of the *West Sussex Gazette*, for his encouragement and in accepting my original articles for the paper. Many thanks also to Portsmouth Publishing and Printing Ltd for their permission to reproduce material from these articles; and to Juliet Pannett for the sketch of George Chant and George Humphries (page 78).

Finally, my grateful thanks to the Weald and Downland Open Air Museum at Singleton for their considerable co-operation in making the publication of this book possible, in particular to Richard Pailthorpe and Christopher Zeuner for their help throughout.

Phœbe Somers
1993

The Weald and Downland Open Air Museum would like to thank West Sussex County Council for its assistance in the publication of this book, and in particular John Godfrey and Kim Leslie.

Photographic Credits

The photographs in the book have been selected to portray scenes and activities contemporary with or typical of those mentioned in the text. It has unfortunately been possible to trace only a few photographs of people or occasions directly referred to. The author is most grateful to all those who have assisted with the photographic research and in particular Richard Pailthorpe, Bob Powell, Peter Jerrome and Martin Hayes. The George Garland photographs are in the ownership of West Sussex County Council and are reproduced by courtesy of the County Archivist.

Jack Beacher, page 3; The National Motor Museum, Beaulieu, page 28; George Garland Collection, West Sussex County Council, pages 6, 7, 15, 17, 19, 20, 21, 27, 31, 35, 37, 41, 43, 45, 46, 47, 48, 49, 53, 65, 67, 71, 73 (bottom); L. Jasper, page 9; Gordon Long, page 40; Littlehampton Museum, pages ii, 60, 61, 62, 63, 73; Richard Pailthorpe, pages 66, 70; Bob Powell, pages 26 (top), 56; Jonathan Roberts, page 13; Ian Serraillier, pages 14, 18, 44, 72 (top), 79; Phœbe Somers, pages 23, 24, 25, 26, 34; Weald and Downland Open Air Museum, pages 32, 39, 57; West Sussex County Council Library Service, pages 5, 30, 51; Barclay Wills, page 76.

Introduction

Once upon a time, so it is said, West Sussex villages were places with large and cheerful families, satisfying work, appetizing food and happy children. The church, the school and the gentry set the rules. The clergy christened, confirmed and comforted, married and buried people who were personally known to them. The school disciplined the children and the gentry gave employment, indoors and out. They helped financially from time to time and showed an interest in all that went on.

So at least it appears to have been when I have talked to country people who were young in the last decade of the nineteenth century and the early part of the twentieth. This seems to confirm that they found satisfaction in their work and their faith in spite of undeniable hardships and discomforts endured in their daily lives, which were run according to accepted patterns.

When all this is compared with the average life of country people today, a wide discrepancy becomes apparent. With very much higher wages bringing such modern conveniences as washing machines, Hoovers, gas, electricity, and laid-on water, all of which allow for a much easier and healthier life, the village scene has virtually changed out of all recognition.

The stories told by these now elderly men and women who have lived into the last quarter of the twentieth century, make a living social history. These people look back nostalgically as they recall the evocative smells of their youth – home-made bread, suet puddings on the boil, lambs, horses, pigs; wet flagstones and clothes hung up in the kitchen to dry.

Despite all efforts to revive it, the old village scene is passing. Such cottages as have remained in the farm workers' care generally retain their original aspect, but a large number have already passed into the hands of retired townsmen, and of weekenders. They house people who have very different backgrounds and standards of living from the original inhabitants and who often show but little interest in the life of the community.

These glimpses into the lives of old country people of two or three generations ago tell us much about hard work, long hours, low wages, poor roads and transport, large families and often great poverty. Yet there was a contentment which, considering the circumstances, is quite surprising.

A Picture of Contentment

'There is no healthier smell than that of sheep in their pens on a frosty morning.' So said Jack Beacher of Aldingbourne, when he was well into his nineties, after shepherding for over fifty years. What words could conjure up a better picture of contentment? Jack went on to say that he often had to go for many days and nights before he could spare the time to return home for a change of clothing. He spent all his time during the lambing season in his shepherd's hut – a wooden contraption, generally on wheels and kept permanently in the lambing fields.

He spoke nostalgically of his life in the open air and ended his reminiscing with the words, 'I still thinks of them – me lambs and me ewes.'

Mr Beacher used his treasured and beautiful crook, which was mounted on a hazel stick. It had been made for him many years previously by Bill Gape, the local blacksmith, who had cleverly created it from a gun barrel.

Mr Beacher had a son, George Alfred John, who found his father to be an exacting teacher when it came to tending sheep. He remembers helping with the marking of young lambs when he was severely ticked off for not holding the stick and the pot of black paint properly, so that the dots were not put in the right places.

He also had a very hard-working mother who, as well as bringing up her four children and doing the countless home and garden jobs, helped to earn a little more money by picking up stones in the flinty Sussex fields. This was really hard work, not only because of the continuous bending. The flints were heavy and wherever they happened to lie had to be carried to the edge of the field and tipped into a bottomless wooden box which held a cubic yard; for this she was paid twopence. As soon as the

Jack Beacher

Jack Beacher with a Southdown ewe

box was filled it had to be lifted and placed elsewhere to await many more refills.

Mrs Beacher also made the most of the local mushrooms of very different kinds and gave her family a change of diet during the season. She put a layer of mushrooms in a large earthenware crock and then a layer of salt, until the vessel was filled. After about three weeks the whole lot was strained and spices and herbs were added.

When the family moved from East Dean to Sompting it was a horse-and-cart affair. The last piece of furniture to be loaded was the settee, balanced on the top, facing forwards, with Mrs Beacher and the children sitting on it. They all thoroughly enjoyed the ride which had started at 8 a.m. and continued until 4 p.m. The sheep-dog ran along under the cart, safely tied between the wheels.

The first combine and baler that Mr Beacher ever saw working on a farm was tractor-drawn, driven from a shaft at the back of the tractor. Another man rode on top to sack off the corn. 'No cab then,' said Mr Beacher, 'you sat in the dust for the rest of the day!'

Findon Sheep Fair

Frank Oliver was another well-known Sussex shepherd. He had a delightful story to tell of an occasion when he had sheared 300 sheep, ready to be driven to Findon Sheep Fair the next day. That evening, however, a large flock of starlings, which had eaten a considerable amount of elderberries, came in among the sheep and left them looking as if they had been dyed blue. This caused great consternation but by the time it was discovered it was too late for anything to be done. Happily, an understanding judge awarded him first prize, in spite of their discoloration.

Another minor disaster was when Frank took 330 sheep from Burpham to West Grinstead. The route led through rough fields and all the animals emerged covered with thousands of burdocks. It would have been quite impossible to have removed them and

Frank Oliver

Frank said that, although they all looked terrible, they managed to fetch a good price. All through his fifty years on the Downs Frank used his great-grandfather's crook, which was regarded as a much-prized heirloom.

Sheep dip by the barrel was one way of doing the job of dipping sheep, making full use of local conditions. This was practised at Splash Farm, Wepham, near Arundel. On the farm there was a natural dip filled from the river Arun. This was known as The Splash. As the river made its way at high tide and filled the dip, it passed through this trough, which had been fenced off to form the dip. As they entered the water the sheep made their way to the far end and were washed by two men suspended in the water. Each man stood up in a barrel which was attached to a post by iron rings. These barrels slipped up and down with the tides, and the sheep, being controlled by the shepherds' crooks, passed between them, being detained long enough to have their wool rubbed by hand. They were then firmly pushed under the water to make their own way to the end of the dip.

Cyril Matcham of Poling said that if the fleeces of his sheep were unusually dirty, the mud balls were easily crushed between two pieces of

Sheep washing in the River Arun at Burpham, near Splash Farm

Findon Sheep Fair, c. 1930

wood and dispersed before the sheep jumped into the dip at the deep end.

In the winter shepherds were employed making hazel hurdles for their sheep-folds, which were sometimes known as deadfolds.

Findon Sheep Fair is still an important feature in the shepherd's year and was looked forward to not only by shepherds but by farmers along with their wives and children. Early this century a day's outing was made of it and a lavish picnic was provided by the wives. On these occasions work and pleasure were inseparable. In the month of September as many as seven or eight thousand sheep were brought to Findon for sale from all over Britain, the vast majority being driven for many miles on foot.

Frank Millam, who lived to see his ninety-ninth birthday, used to leave Burpham at 4 a.m. to drive his sheep some 7 miles across the Downs to Findon Fair, never arriving back home before 10 at night. He had to walk all the way after what must have been an excessively tiring day.

Petworth played an unexpected part in the business of winter sheep-raising, for in the autumns of the last century when Romney Marshes

Shepherds George Chant and George Humphries at Findon Sheep Fair

Driving a flock of Southdown sheep to Findon Sheep Fair

were regularly flooded and the large breeds of sheep there were unable to graze on their usual ground, they were sent to be cared for by Petworth farmers, where they stayed until the following April. The farmers who took them in were known as Kent keepers.

In those days lambs' tails made a cheap and popular meal. They were first stripped and then boiled down to make a thick, and no doubt nutritious, jelly which was a firm favourite with children.

Successful lambing seasons and sheep sales were often celebrated in the pubs by singing the Shepherd's Toast over the beer mugs:

> If I had store
> By sheep and fold
> I'd give you gold.
> But since I'm poor
> By crook and bell
> I wish you well.

A Pig in the Front Room

All the old country people seem to have vivid memories of pigs, for almost every family had at least one. More usually they kept two, one to sell to pay the rent at the end of the year, and the other to feed the family with those well-remembered smoked hams and bacon that formed so large and delicious a part of their diet.

There was an old carter in Poling who thought so much of his pig that when he retired to a small cottage in the village he kept it in his front room. Apparently this kind of treatment was not at all uncommon.

The runts, or undersized last-born of the litter, were sometimes given by the farmer to the poorer families. They were known as 'dolly pigs' and were fattened until they weighed 30 to 40 stones.

Bojam Coombes of Bosham was made responsible when he was quite a small boy, for taking his grandfather's very large pig out on a line to feed on acorns in the woods, thus exercising the right of pannage, an ancient practice dating from the days of Queen Elizabeth I.

As the keeping, killing, salting, smoking and storing of pig meat was of prime importance, every cottager had a slate tank in his garden. Some of these are still to be seen. Fred Goble's parents paid the village postman one shilling and sixpence (7½p) for killing the family pigs, and two shillings (10p) for cutting up the carcases.

A cottage pig

Our Favourite Pudding

With plenty of lard and dripping on hand, dumplings formed a large and much appreciated part of the family meals. Tony Gibbons of Littlehampton had very happy memories of his mother preparing a special dumpling known in the family as a 'swimmer', for which the children competed on their return from school. 'There was a bowl of gravy,' Tony recalled, 'with just one dumpling floating in it. It was lovely and hot and steaming and the first of us to reach home got it. I raced with my eight brothers and sisters, getting home first almost every time. I'm afraid my sisters didn't get much of a chance!'

Mabel Sayers had her memories of the Sunday joint, which was made to go further when her father added a slice of suet pudding to each plate, after it had first been dipped into the hot cooking fat.

'In our day we frequently had just potatoes and bread for our midday meal. Meat was added when it could be afforded. We paid a halfpenny each for herrings and a rabbit could be bought for sixpence (2$\frac{1}{2}$p). Both these formed an important part of our meals, as well as our favourite rolypoly pudding.' Mabel added that blackberries were a much cherished addition when friends, families and school parties went out to gather them every autumn.

What Mrs Caroline Lockyer of Findon called a very important source of food was 'good beef dripping'. She remembered that when carrying out one of her childhood duties, taking a weekly supply of eggs to a neighbour, she was given a basin of 'rich dripping' to take back with her.

One villager remembered that sometimes when she was hungry her mother gave her a large slice of bread and a very small piece of cheese, saying, 'Eat the bread and smell the cheese.' At first the child took this literally and only when her mother found this out did she eat the cheese.

The staple diet was, of course, home-baked wholemeal bread. To quote Jack Burgess of East Preston: 'Delicious smells came from the deep brick bread oven. It was heated by faggots which were kept in a tidy pile outside the kitchen door. The oven held its heat for

Mabel Sayers

several days. My mother made real old-fashioned cottage loaves and she put them into the oven with a large flat wooden paddle. Sometimes boiled potatoes were added to the locally milled flour and such bread never went stale.' He recalled that there was never a day without a cauldron of good soup simmering on the hob.

A Master Flinter

Jack remembered a great deal about his early life which was spent in a large, deeply thatched cottage in Wick, near Littlehampton. It had an exceptionally large larder with wide slate shelves and there was a long slate tank filled with brine for salting the home-killed pig.

The huge old-fashioned fireplace was filled with tree trunks and large branches, which were pushed further and further into the fire as they burned. To the left of this was a special area for smoking the bacon which was hung from large hooks attached to an ancient oak beam up in a loft directly overhead. Access to these was gained by climbing iron staples which were permanently fixed to the wall. Jack waxed lyrical when describing the bread that his mother made in the deep brick oven. 'That was real bread,' he said.

As soon as he left school Jack Burgess started working as a flint knapper with his father, who was a master tradesman-builder. The flint walls of Sussex are well known in the south and Mr Burgess became a master flinter. These walls vary somewhat in style, some being made of rounded stones taken from the beaches. Others, of less regular outlines, were dug out of the fields, mostly by the women, in the eighteenth and nineteenth centuries. It was slow and heavy work and the rewards were small. The stone pickers were paid by the basketful and all stones had to be carried to the edge of the field for later collection by horse and cart.

Jack died in 1982 after a lifetime of flint knapping and wall building. He was very skilled in this difficult and exacting craft and also very knowledgeable in its history. For all those years he constructed these typical Sussex flint walls in a wide area of the county and much of the beauty still left in our villages is due to him.

He had a rather grim story to tell of how, when he was repairing the south chancel wall of Rustington Church, he was surprised and horrified to find, when digging a small ditch just outside, about twenty infants' skulls lying tidily, side by side. There were no written records of these but it is supposed that they were those of stillborn babies of the seventeenth century.

While we are on the subject of flint, it is interesting to note that six cottages at East Hampnett and a few others near by, were built by French prisoners in the Napoleonic wars.

1,000 Bricks a Day

Brick-making was one of the better-paid jobs. All bricks were hand made and were dried in the sun. In the Poling brick works, which turned out chimney-pots, bird baths and flower pots too, Harry Kilgariff remembers that some 900,000 bricks were made annually. Chris Hanks of Didling, another master of the craft, could make his bricks at the rate of two and a half a minute. George Budd working together with another man could turn out 1,000 bricks a day.

The clay was ground by horsepower and the work was quite exhausting, both physically and mentally, for they needed to be aware of every movement they made, and each handful of clay had to be exactly the right size and weight. To pick this amount up at one go was, said Chris, the most difficult part of the training. However, once this was mastered all the men agreed that brick-making was a satisfying job and one of the best available.

As travelling was far less common in those days than it is today, families were much more united. Children made their own games and did their full share of the family chores, both indoors and out; and wives had to be good managers to bring up their families on the husbands' miserably low wages. It seems that not only did sons hand over most of their earnings to their mother but many men passed over their entire wages to their wives, who gave them back a sum considered sufficient for beer and tobacco. It is difficult to see how the women could have managed otherwise, for once a hard-working and thirsty man was inside the pub he wouldn't come out on pay day with much change in his pocket.

The First Tap

Water was often a problem in the farm worker's cottage, for few had it laid on. All the water for a cottage in Wiston had to be fetched from a little fountain at the bottom of quite a steep hill. It must have been no light work carrying the filled buckets back up the hill. It was the responsibility of the families who used the fountain to see that it was cleaned once a week.

Stacking green bricks at Apuldram

A cottage well

To pump up enough water to cool the milk was one of the jobs to be done by James Secomb before he left for school. No water was laid on in his home and in the summer he was sent almost a mile to the River Rother with a water-cart which had a large Portuguese wine barrel fitted to it. This cask was laboriously filled, bucket by bucket, straight from the dyke.

Henry Marten lived in Amberley when water for washing was collected in butts from the roof, and there was a pump in the kitchen. But drinking water was fetched from the River Rother a quarter of a mile away and Henry carried it home in two buckets suspended from a yoke. When he reached his home the water was emptied into large stone crocks kept under the scullery shelves. He was ten years old before he saw his first tap and of this he said, 'It was a source of wonder to me!'

Rob Heasman had home duties of a different kind. For eleven years he was the youngest in the family; then a baby brother was born and Rob had to do a good deal of looking after the new infant. He

Carrying pails suspended from a yoke

remembered pushing the pram with the baby in it and at the same time trying to roll a large stone into the road by manoeuvring it with the front wheels. This had disastrous consequences, as the pram tipped over and the baby fell out. On another occasion he had been forbidden to go to a cricket match at Stopham; instead he was to have kept an eye on the baby at home. But he did see the match, as he ran off taking the baby and pram with him.

Reading Rooms and Self-improvement

'Down towards the end of Poling Street there used to be a reading room,' said Douglas Binstead. 'For a great many years this reading room was the hub of village life but it was demolished in the 1970s and now there is a house built on the site.'

The Duke of Norfolk gave the land for this purpose. The hut had been built by Sam Penn who lived just opposite, in a deeply thatched house called Bacon Hall. When the duke eventually sold the village he

- PHOEBE
SOMERS.

Frank Talbot

presented the reading room to the church for the use of the people in Poling. The subscription was sixpence (2½p) a year and the room was used for billiards, darts and whist drives, as well as being the location of the monthly dinners given to villagers by the local farmers. It was lit by two oil lamps suspended from the ceiling by chains and people used hurricane lamps to light their way to and fro at night. The key was kept by Sam's brother Sid Penn.

Sam and his sister and brother lived at Bacon Hall all their lives and were members of the oldest family in the village. Sam was the village carpenter, wheelwright and undertaker. Some of the villagers remembered that Sam made his own coffin many years before it was needed, and used it as a convenient place in which to store his groceries. When Bacon Hall was renovated after the death of the Penns, a large bacon-smoking area was revealed, built above the main hearth in the old Elizabethan kitchen, and it is supposed that this was the origin of the name of the house.

Frank Talbot, who lived at Northchapel, was a member of a sect known as the Cokelers, also known as the Dependents. This was a religious movement started by one John Sirgood in the early part of the nineteenth century. It was a teetotal group and its nickname derived from its members substituting cocoa for alcoholic drinks. The village of Loxwood became the headquarters of the Dependents and they built a chapel there in 1861.

Tony Gibbons of Littlehampton was a member of the Wick Reading Room Club and he ran a Billiards and Crib League. The two clubs often met at Poling in the evenings, the players walking the 2 miles across fields through Toddington. Tony remembered seeing their lamps swinging in the darkness as they went. Weekly or fortnightly shopping excursions were made on foot from Poling to Wick and Littlehampton. They were usually family affairs and the villagers spread out across the fields, each member carrying two baskets, which were generally of the old-fashioned fishnet kind.

Village Celebrations

Village celebrations seem to have made an indelible impression on the minds of children and one of Archie Farley's most glowing memories, treasured by him well into his eighties, was of the festivities arranged to celebrate the safe return of the Duke of Norfolk from the Boer War. 'There were hundreds of coloured lights and a great display of fireworks on the lake in Arundel Park. We had free ices, drinks and cigarettes,' he recalled with evident pleasure.

Another highlight was the celebration of Queen Victoria's Diamond Jubilee. When Archie was aged eleven he was taken to the fields next to Arundel Station, to see the passing of the old queen's funeral train.

Arundel came in for regattas, torchlight processions and, of course, the Goodwood traffic. This caused a great deal of excitement locally, as the four-in-hands passed through the town carrying the more wealthy racegoers from Brighton to Goodwood. Ordinary cabs took the less wealthy people there the day before and waited at Chichester until the last

May Day celebrations, Amberley, 1929

Goodwood Races during the 1920s

day of the races. To quote Archie Farley once again: 'During Goodwood Week it was the custom for us small boys to waylay the four-in-hands as they passed through Arundel on the return journey to Brighton, and to follow them for as many miles as we were capable of running. All the time we were calling out, as often and as loudly as our breath would allow, "Throw out your rusty coppers! Throw out your rusty coppers!"' Gratifying showers of coins kept them going for several miles.

During his few years at school Archie earned threepence a week for taking breakfast to the men who were rebuilding the castle at that time.

Schooldays

Mabel Sayers, whose mother fed and clothed her family during the First World War on her army allowance of sixteen shillings (80p) a week while her husband was away at the front, has happy memories of her childhood, but when compared to the lives of children today, they make harsh reading.

Fetching water in Amberley

'My sister and I,' said Mrs Sayers, 'were sent fairly regularly to walk the one and a half miles into Arundel Station to fetch a sack of coal – which cost one shilling and sixpence (7½p) – and push it all the way back up the steep hill in a little two-wheeled orange box. We had to do this before school, which started at 9 a.m. After school there was the next day's wood to be collected, as well as a bucket of water from the pump. This pump was fenced off and belonged to the Duke of Norfolk, who gave a key to each family entitled to use it.'

Joe Tuesley worked after school as delivery boy. When lessons were over at 4 p.m. he pushed a handcart of groceries taking goods to houses up to 5 miles away. He did further deliveries all day on Saturdays, earning three shillings (15p) a week. Out of this he gave his mother two shillings and sixpence (12½p) for his keep, spending the remaining sixpence (2½p) chiefly on cinema seats at a penny halfpenny a time.

Winifred Berryman used to deliver milk at certain homes on her way to school, collecting the empty cans on her way back home. Leslie Warner remembered with but little pleasure a seemingly endless 2½ miles walk to school, and then the same walk back at the end of the day.

Sawing wood

Caroline Lockyer of Findon said she caught all the infectious childish diseases going, including diphtheria and scarlet fever. At the age of five she showed a talent for music and was taught to play the piano with pennies resting on the backs of her hands. 'I was also taught to sing and to play chants,' she remembered. 'My teacher used to leave me in the room to get on with the playing while she did her cooking down in the basement, calling up the stairs at intervals: "Do more singing. It isn't worth tuppence if you don't sing!"'

Miss Winifred Allen who eventually became headmistress of Amberley Church of England School, had an early recollection of when she was three or four years old. The Rector of Storrington, the Revd George Faithful,

Winifred Allen

Children helping on the farm

who was very old and frail, went about in a pony-drawn bathchair. He used to call in his bathchair at her home from time to time, to discuss church matters with her father, who was a church-warden. On leaving, Mr Faithful always asked for 'the little maid' and took her into the bathchair back to the rectory, where she was given a biscuit with strawberry jam on it.

The village schoolmaster has come in for a good deal of criticism and was the subject of many jokes as well as rueful memories. Said Bill Wills of Blakehurst, of his headmaster: 'He was a terror in school and a gentleman out of it.' Admitting that no boy played truant more than he, perhaps he had good reason to fear his master, though he added, 'It was worth it, even with the tanning.'

Walter Lillywhite of Eartham said that his headmaster was not a suitable type to have been put in charge of children. But Walter had reason to be grateful to Eartham School, for it was over the playground wall that on his very first day he saw and spoke to the girl he was eventually to marry.

Tom Gumbrell

Bill Skinner of Houghton said that after a caning at school he was given another by his father when he got home; and George Budd well remembered that his headmaster owned a walking-stick which was quickly brought into action when occasion demanded.

William (Speedo) Paine of Bosham was much in awe of his early teachers, Mrs Keatley and Mrs Peat, both of whom wore long black skirts and had their hair in ringlets. Talking of his headteacher at Lancastrian Boys' School in Chichester, he said, 'He was certainly a stern old fellow.'

Tom Gumbrell of West Chiltington started school at the very early age of three and he recalled that, during the next eleven years, he had his share of the cane. He was familiar with the command, 'Bend down and touch your toes!'

William Stone of Lancing had a happier tale to tell, for he was taught by a very popular headmistress, Miss Humphries. On her ninety-third birthday he and several other of Miss Humphries' old pupils attended a reception given in her honour. At the party her hosts gave her two things – a large bouquet and a small cane. Still talking of Miss Humphries, William continued: 'On Friday afternoons during the last lesson of the week she would read a few chapters of some special book. On one of these Fridays before starting to read to us she said that she would give the book to the best-behaved boy when it was finished. I tried very hard and I won it. That was sixty-two years ago, and although I have lost other boyhood treasures, I have managed to keep that book. Last week it turned up in my bookcase and inside I found a pressed forget-me-not. I think Miss Humphries must have put it in as the book has never been out of my possession. She was a great teacher and she taught us how to behave. Many of us had much to thank her for.'

The general consensus of opinion of these pupils of village schools was: 'If we broke the rules we got what we deserved. It didn't do us any harm; it was a reminder of what was right and what was wrong.'

Miss Margery Ellis of Pulborough gave the picture from the other side. 'I was very young when I qualified,' she said. 'I started off with a

The village school, East Hoathly

class of seventy-two "mixed infants" and I was expected to control them.' Near by she kept handy a black rod, covered by a green cloth. All the children knew it was there and the mere threat to use it worked wonders. Miss Ellis had three main subjects – botany, geography and needlework – but she was expected to teach many others as well.

No one should have been expected to work in the conditions she had to. To begin with she wasn't made at all welcome by the three other teachers already installed. No chair was provided for her during school hours so, to get off her feet, she had to sit on the rail of the fireguard. 'It was a bit hot at times,' she remembered, 'and eventually it burnt out the back of my skirt!' The schoolroom fire was used during the winter dinner hours by the children to roast the large potatoes they brought with them for their lunches.

Out of her sparse salary Miss Ellis paid for her lodgings and her keep. The day came when she decided to treat herself to a new hat and to pay for this she handed over her entire monthly salary, receiving back just one penny in change!

The village school, Coolham

As well as carrying out her teaching duties Miss Ellis was the instigator of the school dinners, cooking and serving the meals herself. Three paraffin stoves were used and there was no water supply. She planned a different dinner for every day of the month and the children were charged fourpence, out of which a small profit was made. Quite often she and the other teachers would remain in school long after hours, to bottle fruit and do other voluntary jobs. Eventually Miss Ellis became the headmistress of this school, and a very good one she must have been. Referring to the general atmosphere of teaching in those days, Miss Ellis said, 'There was nothing sinister or unpleasant, there were no nasty elements – just high spirits.'

It was expected that even tiny children should walk to school whatever the distance. Walter Lillywhite at the age of five covered the 3½ miles of rough lanes and ploughed fields in all weathers, and there was trouble if he didn't arrive with clean and shining boots. At the age of four, Gladys Baker of North Mundham was dragged very

The village school, East Preston

unwillingly the 2½ miles to school, along rough flint roads, wearing heavy, uncomfortable boots. The old shepherd Jack Beacher used to walk 2 miles each way to Standean School, every yard of it across ploughed fields.

Mrs Nellie Skinner who lived in Findon village all her life, started school at the very early age of two. This, of course, was exceptional but the schools were generally ready to help mothers who themselves had to start working for other people first thing in the morning. Under the same arrangements Bill Skinner and Mrs Lillian Knight both started school when they were three and Douglas

Nellie Skinner

The family goat

Caplan was accepted when he was four.

Sometimes the luckier schoolchildren rode home in farm wagons or on the broad unsaddled backs of the great Shire horses. Gilbert Bannister went to a school so remote that in bad weather only a very few children were expected to turn up. He walked there from a home that was so tucked away in the Downs that his mother sometimes saw no other woman for six months at a time.

Families generally kept at least one goat, and many had more. However, if they lived near the school, they could be an awful nuisance. In the first place they had

Mr Charles Boxall from Wisborough Green delivering milk, c. 1910

Loading milk churns at Selham Station

to be milked by one of the children before school, and then pegged down in the lane or in a nearby field.

Sid Reeves's family owned a very obstinate pair of nannies which far too often escaped from their tethers and made their way directly to the school. They sought out Sid by appearing and bleating at his classroom window. This always created a welcome diversion, though perhaps not so much for Sid. When the goats were in this mood he had to soothe them at milking time by wearing his grandmother's skirt in order to calm them down with the right scent.

When Florence Greenfield of Storrington spoke of her schooldays she ruefully remembered the milk churns, for she travelled daily by bus from Storrington Station to Worthing in the company of those hard, rattling objects which had to be picked up at the station and put into the main body of the bus. Passengers had to arrange themselves round them, often having to sit with a knee at either side. She has never forgotten the clatter of those empty churns as they jogged about on the floor of the bus.

The First Cars

As a boy Reg Davison had an absorbing interest in cars. He learnt to handle those early models which seldom arrived at their destination without mishap. Breakdowns were frequent, dusty roads often proved hazardous and tyres were expected to be cut to pieces by flint and grit. At the age of fifteen Reg could drive and in 1911, when he was seventeen, he was put in full charge of his employer's first car, a Panhard.

The early Panhard had quadrant-change gears, no windscreen wiper and a handbrake on the outside, which had to be pushed to be brought into action.

A 1908 Panhard. Note the snake-like horn above the running-board

'The car was entered from the back,' Reg explained 'and the snake-like horn which ran the length of the running-board was worked by air pressure induced by squeezing a rubber bulb, which forced air through a set of reeds. These reeds didn't last long and constantly needed replacement, so we also carried a klaxon horn.'

The sides and back of the car were lit by oil lamps and the headlights by acetylene. This car, which had no battery, ran off a magneto; it had wooden wheels and the tyres were kept in place by four security bolts held inside by shoulders and pins. Two huge spare wheels with tyres were strapped to the running-board.

The next car to come into Reg's care was a Humber which started up on a 4 volt battery kept on the running-board, which automatically switched over to the magneto when ready. His third car was a Sunbeam.

'I found,' said Reg, 'this Sunbeam had very complicated electrical fittings, with some of the wires running underneath the mudguards and along the entire length of the chassis. Its maintenance was by no means simple; young as I was, I was responsible for all repairs including such things as relining the brakes. For this job I was supplied with a sheet of brake-lining material which was covered with brass filings. Strips of this very rough stuff were cut out to size for the brake shoes, then drilled, counter-sunk and riveted. It was very hard on my knuckles which were often sore and bleeding. Also the removing and replacing of the frequently punctured tyres added to the soreness. Every week these cars had to be oiled and greased thoroughly, and there was a great deal of brass to be polished daily.'

Kirdford had its own postman, Ron Snelling. Ron was the first man in the village to own a motor-cycle but this was not used for delivery of letters. For that he was supplied with a bicycle and his uniform. But he had to buy his own boots.

Ron's father had to deliver goods in London in what was known as 'a broad-wheeled wagon'. This vehicle had two iron rings on each wheel and was driven between Kirdford and London when there were only twisting lanes between the village and Guildford Turnpike.

Ron Snelling

Tom Honeybun

Like most postmen, Ron suffered from many attacks by dogs. Once he lost the seat of his trousers and on another occasion he was taken to hospital for treatment. Many country people were illiterate, so Ron was sometimes asked to read their letters to them, and even occasionally to write their replies. 'But,' he said, 'I generally used to dodge that!'

Another postman with long service was Tom Honeybun who was born at Ham, near Sidlesham. He joined the Post Office staff at Barnham in 1920 and worked in it for the next thirty-one years. At first he did his rounds on foot; later one bicycle was provided to be

Bury Hill

shared with the head postman. As this man was tall and Tom was short, this sharing involved changing the height and position of the saddle every time they changed over.

Two hazards faced them on every workday. The bad roads were full of pot-holes and they were often thrown from their bike in cold and slippery weather. The other danger was from dogs and they sometimes suffered quite serious injury.

Frank Millam, who died only a few weeks before his hundredth birthday, owned a Rover 8 in 1911 which needed a good deal of upkeep. Frank claimed to be the first man to drive a cattle lorry up Bury Hill. This lorry, and indeed most cars, had to be put into reverse gear in order to climb the hill. It was the lowest gear and the only one able to deal with the gradient.

Harry Espin, who for forty years was stud groom to the Duke of Norfolk, was brought into service by the words 'Come and walk me a yearling'. He remembered the great nervousness of his horses when the first cars came on to the roads. They were known as 'chitterbugs' which perhaps tells us all we need to know of the noise they created. Accidents were frequent and compensation virtually nil.

Cattle auction, Pulborough Market, 1934. Note the lorries in the background

Job Satisfaction

Countrymen were experienced in a remarkably large number of varied jobs and skills. This was largely due to lack of serious training for any one craft; but the system (if it could be called that) certainly produced men who could turn their hands to work as diverse as those of their capable wives who were bringing up the children at home. Those who were farm workers, blacksmiths, builders or flint knappers, cobblers, postmen, fishermen, or housemaids who lived to reach their seventies, eighties, or nineties expressed a genuine love of the past. What is now called 'job satisfaction' is recognized today as one of the keys to happiness. It is possible that the many different skills then expected of the country people prevented staleness and boredom. There were always things to be done and seasons in which to do them. A farm which today may need only three or four men, would have employed perhaps as many as twenty-three or twenty-four.

On such days as were too cold, wet, or muddy to get on with the outside work, there were large barns for jobs which could be done inside.

A wimble for twisting straw ropes

In the barns there was companionship and work such as mangel-cutting, shovelling roots or milling corn for the cattle. There were many opportunities and plenty of time for jokes and gossiping. The community was self-contained and this paved the way to shared interests and general contentment.

One of the crafts practised in the barns during inclement weather was making string for tying up 36 pound straw trusses. This was done by using strands of loose hay which were twisted on a 'wimble' – a Z-shaped device made of stout wire, with an ash or willow handle at one end. This was turned by one man while a second man fed it at the other end by twisting the hay into a strong cord. The man turning the wimble walked backwards as the string lengthened.

On wet days men protected themselves by covering their shoulders with old sacks; once they were wet they stayed wet, for no such luxuries as wellingtons or mackintoshes existed.

A Crop of Accidents

Said Fred Osborne of Yapton: 'Before I became a regular railroad worker on the London, Brighton and South Coast Railway I had worked as stableboy, coal carrier, polisher of antique silver, cleaner of boots, knives and forks, farm boy and gardener.' He then achieved his ambition of becoming an engine cleaner. While he was awaiting his call to the engine sheds Fred undertook yet another job in a munitions factory.

He gave a vivid account of a near-accident he had in the engine shed not long after he had been appointed as a cleaner. 'Whenever the engine was being cleaned,' he said, 'notices had to be placed both before and behind it, bearing the words "NOT TO BE MOVED." This was a safety precaution and a warning to drivers who were moving rolling stock to keep well away from the area so that the cleaner could concentrate on the job in hand. I remember,' he continued, 'that once, when I was well underneath the engine, I heard a pilot approaching and in a few seconds I managed to wriggle down through the "motions" into the pit just in time to avoid being injured in the inevitable crash!'

Another railway incident that might well have turned out badly was witnessed, and never forgotten, by Mrs Shepherd, also of Yapton. At the level crossing she saw a runaway truck careering swiftly down the line, empty and out of control. Luckily it ran itself safely into a siding.

– PHŒBE
SOMERS –

Jack Hampshire

At his house in Crossbush, Jack Hampshire, that giant of the world of steam, told me how, as a young man, he survived a very nasty accident while working under a steam wagon which had been set up on blocks with its wheels removed. Describing the scene he said, 'I thought my eyes were playing tricks but what was happening was that the whole thing was sliding to one side. Bent double, I was trapped beneath it with only 18 inches to live in. My back was well and truly scraped but eventually the mass was jacked up to release me. Even today I bear heavy scars on my back.'

In Arundel, Carlo Lawrence told how he ran into difficulties in quite another

A traction-engine accident at Lidsey, 1923

way. In June 1949 he earned the Certificate of the Royal Humane Society for saving two people from drowning in the River Arun. A skiff was out of control in a swiftly receding tide just above Arundel Bridge and two people were thrown into the river. Carlo, a non-swimmer, ran along the bank, jumped in and grabbed them both, and managed to bring them safely to shore.

Accidents with cattle were very frequent and no fewer than four times did George Taylor manage to escape unharmed after being knocked over, or chased by a bull. The last time that happened he had to vault a 4 foot door into a stable. The bull was following very close behind him and broke the door open. George was bent down behind it and got somewhat squashed but eventually managed to get out safely.

Ernest Sopp told an uncomfortable story of an occasion when he was riding a colt which, as soon as it felt the turf beneath its hooves, got the bit between its teeth and bolted, galloping a considerable distance to the bottom of the park. Approaching a five-barred gate Ernest hoped that the animal would stop there long enough to give him the chance to throw himself off. But no such thing happened. The colt raced on

A prize-winning beast at Pulborough Fat Stock Show in the 1920s

- PHŒBE SOMERS -

Charlie Roberts

towards a wall and Ernest feared it would try to jump over – feared because he knew, but the colt didn't, there was a 7 foot drop the other side. Fortunately the animal slipped on the wet turf and came to an abrupt stop at the foot of the wall and hesitated just long enough for Ernest to slip off. Leading the colt back, he was met by the owner who had witnessed the whole episode and was as relieved as Ernest himself to see the happy ending, when the chances had been so much against it.

There are always plenty of incidents on a farm and Charlie Roberts of Warningcamp remembers one in which an old black mare called Polly managed to get herself caught between two trees growing close together. When he found her struggling she had clearly been there 'a tidy while'. The question was how to extricate her. It was decided that a saw be fetched to cut away part of one of the trees. This done, the mare walked off with no damage other than being 'a bit scrased'.

An account of another near accident was told by Wilf Vinson of Bignor. When he was clearing hedges and chopping wood on the top of a high bank opposite his cottage, the axe flew off its handle and went careering down into the lane below. Luckily no one was passing at the time.

Service Overseas

A surprising number of men and women from rural Sussex joined up during the two wars, despite the fact that they were usually in a reserved occupation. Suddenly they were lifted out of their familiar surroundings into the strangeness of foreign countries, and the hazards and discomforts of total war. They found themselves in Egypt, Salonika, Macedonia, Serbia, Bulgaria, Turkey, Burma, France and Germany, as well as in many other parts of the world. Men and women who might never have expected to leave their own immediate environment were faced with serving in the armed forces with all that it entailed.

Harry Espin, who became the Duke of Norfolk's head groom, was one of those who joined up in the 1914–18 war and he recalled with

Armistice Day; remembering fallen comrades

amusement an occasion when, while on active service between Baghdad and Turkey, and having ridden on horseback for over 500 miles, he found that the seat of his breeches was worn completely through. Being resourceful, he cut off a corner of his tunic and applied it to the relevant areas with a bootlace.

Kath Reeves, whose family worked in the service of the Dukes of Norfolk for generations, joined the forces and ran canteens in Burma for eighteen months in the Second World War. After the war she continued her driving, delivering groceries to the villages scattered round the vicinity of Arundel.

Art of the Wheelwright

The old Sussex name of Woolgar has been well known in Steyning from at least as far back as 1840 when Mr Harold Woolgar's grandfather started up a successful wheelwright's workshop.

Harold Woolgar

Mr Woolgar was one of six children. He was born in 1903 and attended the Church of England school. He left on his fourteenth birthday and started work the next morning at 6 o'clock. It was obvious that he should go into the family business in which he stayed for the rest of his working life.

All work in the yards was done by hand and it was heavy and tiring for a lad. Standing trees were bought to supply the necessary timber and these were cut down with large hatchets and saws.

Heavy horses were hired from neighbouring farms and the trees were transported on huge timber wheels. Each horse could easily haul as much as 2 tons.

The ash, oak and elm were cut up with a two-man saw over a 7 feet deep pit, and young Harold was put at the bottom, raising and lowering his arms for thirty minutes at a time.

Mr Woolgar's father, Charles, improved the strength of the wagon body by inventing a tapered tenon used on the main timbers.

With each wagon being of individual design, a Sussex wheelwright could tell who had made any particular model.

On three wagons Mr Woolgar made with the assistance of only one other wheelwright and one carpenter, each pair of staves was worked out at a different angle to accommodate the lade and the boarding.

It would take two or three men five months to construct a full-sized wagon. The result was probably not recognized as a masterpiece then, but has certainly come into its own as such with the passing of the years.

Woolgars used to make all the large heavy drays for the Steyning Breweries and for many years they were part of the local scene.

Mr Woolgar showed me one of the most beautiful books I have ever handled. It is a pattern book for various types of carts and it has the family name printed on the outer cover. Published about 140 years ago, on thick, smooth paper, its elegant delineations portray carts of many kinds; it was from this book that the men of the Woolgar family took the designs for their bakers' vans, butchers' buggies, milk floats, tip carts and drays, to mention only a few.

A model farm cart

Mr Woolgar had, as might be expected, made some very fine models of Sussex wagons with every detail perfect, including his father's tapered tenons.

The Heavy Horses

James Colwell worked at Eartham for many years. His Shires, Suffolk Punches and Clydesdales so dominated his life that when he left farming to go into the building industry, he found that he couldn't do without them, so after only a short time at his new job he returned to his team on the farm and was happy once again.

In his retirement Mr Colwell relived his satisfying life by making some splendid models. He turned a garage at the back of his cottage into a little museum. There he displayed his beautifully made scale models of carts, caravans, timber nibs, tip carts, scotch carts, four-wheeled wagons, coal carts and one old-type dust cart. Each vehicle had the right type of horse in the shafts.

Apart from being 'dressed' for horse shows, it was far more common then for the heavy horses on a farm to be beautified by highly polished brass ornaments, coloured ribbons and the art of mane and tail plaiting,

Heavy horses pulling a timber wagon

known as 'tracing'. Tracing is a craft which is tremendously complicated and exacting, in which Cyril Matcham, Bill Wills and James Colwell were all experts.

Bill Wills

The sagacity of the heavy horse is quite remarkable and Bill Wills told of an incident that took place in Arundel Park when he was working in the woods. Bill became aware of some impending disaster through the odd behaviour of his team: the horses suddenly refused to take another step forward. Try as he might, they wouldn't budge, and it eventually transpired that, quite out of sight but right in their path, some large trees had fallen, completely blocking the work in hand.

Bill told me that a Shire horse could pull a load five times its own weight. 'I always gave mine a treat every Saturday and they learnt to expect it,' he said. 'It

A ploughman and his team taking a break from harrowing

Harvesting mangel-wurzels

was a mixture of linseed and bran mash and they became restless and excited when they smelt and heard it being prepared. Another treat they had was when the mangel-wurzels were "withery and mellow", I used to throw some into the stable for them and that gave me pleasure just to listen to them being chewed and enjoyed.'

Many of the old horsemen I chatted with had their own ideas about horses which had white markings on their legs. Bill quoted a rhyme which neatly settled the matter, in just four lines.

> One white leg – buy him.
> Two white legs – try him.
> Three white legs – doubt him.
> Four white legs – do without him.

His other version was:

> Four white legs – give him away.
> Three white legs – don't keep him a day.
> Two white legs – give him to a friend.
> One white leg – keep him to the end.

Ploughing the Fields

The distances these horsemen walked behind their heavy horses when ploughing were considerable. Jesse Feast of Midhurst remembered the days when he followed Sailor and Stormer root-hoeing and he reckoned he covered every bit of 11 miles a day.

Jesse Feast

John Horn of Climping, a past master of ploughing, gave a graphic description of the intricacies of the measuring necessary to plough a straight furrow. 'There were two things that should never be allowed to be overlooked,' he said. One was that the two great animals had to be placed a certain number of paces from the edge of the field right at the beginning of the first furrow. The second was the absolute necessity of being able to turn the whole contraption at exactly the

Ploughing beneath Chanctonbury Ring

right place in the field. 'You had to start right,' he explained, 'or else it would go wrong all the way.' John pointed out that the last furrow of all, which was 6 feet wide and 6 inches deep, was the most difficult of the lot to manoeuvre. 'You see,' he explained, 'it had to fit in with those on either side. If they weren't in line you can imagine what it would look like!' He, too, reckoned that he walked between 10 and 11 miles a day behind his team.

David Emmett, who lived in a very old cottage in Bignor Park, said he would like to know how many hundreds of miles he must have walked behind his horses. His day began at 6 a.m. and ended with racking up at 7 p.m. 'It was nosebags all round at midday and we had a second break between 3 and 3.30.'

David remembered that for the harvesting three old Sussex wagons were used, each with three Shire horses in the shafts. Twenty-five sacks of threshed corn were put on each wagon and taken from Lee Farm to Angmering Station. On the return journey the wagons were loaded with steam coal which came straight from the pit-head and cost one shilling (5p) per hundredweight. This was used throughout the winter for threshing by steam engine.

A Sussex wagon at Bignor

Harvesting on the Downs

Wilf Whiffen, a Worthing man, told of the wisdom – or perhaps it should be called the cunning – of a horse in his charge in the 1914–18 war. This was a wily beast which, from time to time, challenged Wilf in a contest of craftiness, for one of his favourite tricks was to free himself from his stall. It was some time before Wilf found out how he did it. The horse needed the assistance of the occupant of the next stall; the procedure was then quite simple. The neighbouring horse nibbled at Wilf's horse's head-dress until it became loose, then all he had to do was to shake his head, back out and trot off!

On leaving school a farm worker's son very often joined his father as carter boy. Frank Whittington of Burpham at the age of thirteen was, on his second day, put to a two-horse plough all by himself – no easy task, even for a trained man. He said that to turn the horses on the hillside was fraught with difficulty and danger, and he remembered being very apprehensive about it.

Taking advice from an old hand on adjusting the plough

Bill Kilhams

Bill Kilhams of Bury Farm, where he spent the whole of his working life, was put in charge of a four-horse team for ploughing when he was only seventeen. He spoke of Jolly, Captain, Prince and Steamer with pride and affection, saying: 'All horses know who is their master; they have their own ways of showing recognition and also that they are pleased to see him.'

What these young boys learnt was never forgotten, as was made clear by Cyril Matcham of Poling. Cyril started working on the farm when he was only eleven years of age, and he continued until he was well over seventy. When he was over eighty he could still recite all the drill for getting his Suffolk Punches into the shafts. 'The first thing to do,' he said, 'was to slip the collars over the horses' heads and then wait for orders.' One nice little touch that Cyril remembered was that the men's wives used to make earcaps for the horses. Flies were a real nuisance and caused much distress to the animals and these little caps were some protection. They were made from calico and were decorated with red, white and blue tassels, which, he said, 'dangled and swung with each movement'.

George Trussler worked for over forty years on Stakers Farm, Yapton, and one of his memories was of how the great horses, as soon as their harness was removed at the end of the day, would make their own way to the meadows where they were free to roam, graze and roll to their heart's content. This had a beneficial effect on the summer grooming as the animals would clean themselves by rolling luxuriously in the grass.

Harrowing on the Downs

Owen Crowhurst

The Village Blacksmith

Owing to the rough and flinty condition of the Sussex roads at the turn of the century, wear and tear on horses' shoes was considerable, and that's where the village blacksmith comes into the picture. Two of the best known of the West Sussex blacksmiths were Frank Brasington ('Only one S in my name; my father couldn't afford two!') of Storrington, and Owen Crowhurst of Amberley. Owen was one of four brothers who were all blacksmiths, as was their father, and he spent his life among horses as much as

Fittleworth Forge in the 1930s

Shoeing a horse at Fittleworth Forge

if he had been a carter on a farm. He must have had a most remarkable memory, for it was never necessary for him to write down any of the various types, sizes and measurements connected with the shoeing of the many animals with which he dealt. Once he had made a set of shoes for a horse the measurements remained in his memory for further reference.

When Frank Brasington retired he still plied his craft, occupying his time making such things as candlesticks, wrought-iron gates and pokers. 'After fifty-four years,' he said, 'you can't just let it go.'

Another well-known Sussex blacksmith was Ted Agate of Wepham, who said that throughout his many years of smithing, he was never actually kicked by a horse, but often kicked at; and he was thrown out of a stable more than once by an unco-operative animal. Ted also told of a donkey whose feet were badly in need of trimming. He picked up one of its front legs ready to begin. He held it between his knees in the usual way, but the donkey took charge, walking around taking Ted with him, with the result that the shoeing took two and a half hours to complete!

Fighting Fires

At the turn of the century horses were still being relied on to be put into the shafts of the fire engines. These animals were not kept specifically for fighting fires; they were also used for other purposes and in a fire emergency they had to be sought out from wherever they happened to be at the time, put into the shafts and driven to the site of the fire at whatever speed they could muster.

A large fire at Bury House, in the village of Bury, caused a great deal of excitement on 20 April 1909. The old house was almost completely destroyed. The cause of the outbreak was never discovered, though its origin was eventually traced to the old roof timbers. It all started at 11 a.m. and the flames spread rapidly; within an hour the old building was practically gone.

Three fire engines were summoned by telegraph from the nearby post office. Arundel was the first to receive the signal which arrived at eleven minutes past the hour. Fortunately, the horses weren't out working that day, so they were quickly collected from a field and harnessed to the town engine – and what an exciting run it must have been with the steep and winding slopes of Bury Hill to manoeuvre. It must have called for great control and horsemanship.

Bury village

Arundel Castle's private fire brigade, 1910

The Petworth Fire Brigade had also been called and it arrived quite soon in spite of the distance being greater than that from Arundel. By then yet another urgent call had been telegraphed, this time to Arundel Castle, asking for help from the Duke of Norfolk's brigade.

Having got the horses and engines together on site, the next thing to be organized was water. Supplies were available from two sources: first a pond, which was behind the house, and then the River Arun, which was about a quarter of a mile away. For the rest of the day the firemen worked unceasingly, not only to try to save the house but also to prevent the fire spreading to the old post office stores and some ancient thatched cottages just on the other side of the road. The old buildings and the thatched roofs were soaked and resoaked with the hosed water, the men not deeming it safe to leave until every sign of smoke and smouldering had died down.

Dan Baker of Arundel remembered a curious appliance which was kept opposite his home. It was a mobile fire escape which was manned by volunteers. When a fire broke out it was rushed, propelled by hand, to be set up beneath the windows of the burning building.

Working Dogs

Stories about dogs abound, farmers and gamekeepers having to depend on their dogs to help in many ways.

Fred Goble's collie would run out by himself every morning, often before dawn, into the fields to find the cows which were lying in the shelter of the hedges and would bring in each one safely.

Bill Skinner

Bill Skinner, a gamekeeper, had a favourite Springer named Chum which went everywhere with him. He also had two black Labradors and one day one of these, Nigger by name, didn't come to heel at the end of the day, as was his custom. Nigger had last been seen at the edge of the woods some distance away from his usual area. After much calling and whistling Bill had to return without him. By the time he got back it was quite dark. None of the family had seen Nigger, so after the evening meal they all set out to help with the search, spreading out through the woods where the dog had last been seen. As this was beyond the normal working areas, it was probably out of earshot, but as the searchers approached, Nigger was seen sheltering against a hedge, patiently waiting to be given the accustomed order which allowed him to leave.

Mr Boaz Cornford of Clapham was returning from Hailsham Market with his dog which he had sent on ahead to control the cattle. Suddenly and quite unexpectedly, the dog jumped through an open window, tumbling everything off the owner's breakfast table!

Mr Cornford had an amusing anecdote which concerned his childhood. When the cartload of full milk churns made its daily journey to the station, the empty churns from the previous day were collected to be brought back to the farm. If he had behaved well the day before, the young Boaz was allowed to travel home inside one of the churns. Mr Cornford, when I knew him, was a large man and I found it difficult to imagine his ever having been small enough to get inside a churn!

A farmer's collie dog

The Cobbler

Many villagers had their own boot and shoe makers and menders; Alec Rogers of Lodsworth was one of them. He and his wife Ruth lived in what used to be the old post office and it was here that the first telegram to arrive brought news of the relief of Kimberley on 12 February 1901.

From the age of seven Alec sang in the church choir and he remembered the joy of the choir boys when the sexton used to throw his cap up at the large number of bats when they flew all over the church during evening choir practice.

Mr Rogers lost a leg in the fighting in France when he was only nineteen. On his return home he trained in bootmaking and repairing and he eventually set up in Lodsworth. For making ladies' shoes he charged thirty shillings (£1.50) and for men's shoes he charged fifty shillings (£2.50). Alec remembered one resident bringing him some buckskin breeches, asking for them to be made into a pair of shoes. This challenge resulted in one pair of cricket boots, one pair of tennis shoes and one pair of walking shoes.

Alec's parents came from Petworth where his great-uncle was Police Constable No. 1 and his father Police Constable No. 13. Several items of their uniform are now in the Police Museum in Chichester.

Women's Work

It was usual for the girls in a farm worker's family to go into domestic service at about the age of fourteen and sometimes even earlier, though this was the exception.

Those who went on to become ladies' maids sometimes came into contact with distinguished house guests. Mrs Ruth Rogers, wife of Alec the shoemaker, told me with some glee of her experiences when she was in the service of Lady Cunliffe who lived in the hamlet of River, near Midhurst. When attending Lady Cunliffe on a visit to the Gladstones at Hawarden Castle in Flintshire she was dared by one of the housemaids to put on Mr Gladstone's ceremonial hat, which was hanging in the hall. This she immediately did. On turning round to show the back she was horrified to find herself face to face with the Duke of Connaught. It was clear from the duke's expression what he was thinking but, after a moment's hesitation, he passed on in disapproving silence.

Another of Mrs Rogers' memories of staying in large houses with her employer in her capacity of lady's maid, was of a visit to Knole in Kent, the home of the Sackvilles. She always looked forward to those visits where she was well received by the resident domestic staff. At the end of the day she was seen safely to her room by a watchman who lit the way with a hurricane lamp.

Aged ninety-four and spending her last years in very comfortable accommodation at Wisborough Green, Mrs Alice Marsh left school when she was only ten. For the next four years she stayed at home to help her mother with the large and ever growing family.

Alice Marsh

'At home,' she said, 'we just ran wild. Our mother always seemed to have a new baby in her arms and she had little time to see what we were up to. If any mischief was afoot, I was in it!'

As soon as she was fourteen, Alice went into domestic service and confessed that she was glad to get away from the large and boisterous family, to enjoy the comparative peace. Her first post was in a large house in Brighton, where she had a good time with the other servants, some of whom were as young as herself. Alice recalled such larks as trying on a series of top hats one evening, when the owners were dining. While she was doing this she became aware of someone watching her as a voice called out, 'Don't any of them fit you, Alice?'

From private service Mrs Marsh went on to Cranleigh School where she was the linen maid. All the domestic staff were expected to attend chapel on Sundays and Alice remembered an occasion when she decided not to go. Sitting in her room, enjoying her freedom, she suddenly heard the matron's heels clicking along the corridor as she searched out the absent ones. Quick as lightning Alice leapt into bed, shoes and all, pleading sickness. 'It worked!' she said joyfully. 'It really worked!'

Mrs Gladys Baker, whose first job at the age of fourteen was kitchen maid at Salt Hill House, Fishbourne, soon learnt all about hard work and long hours, although she was perfectly happy working under a kindly and good-tempered cook. She was up at 6 every morning, raking

Domestic staff from a country house

out the enormous old kitchen stove. She then lit the fire ready for the cook to come down and make the wholemeal scones for breakfast. Then she prepared the cook's table for baking, putting out the pastry board, rolling pin and all the other necessities. Gladys was also responsible for cleaning the long ground-floor passages on both sides of the green baize door.

This was followed by cleaning and tidying the cook's and lady's maid's bedrooms and scrubbing the back stairs. After that it was time to do seasonable jobs such as game preparation and rabbit skinning, or stoning plums for jam. Another duty was to lay the table in the servants' hall, to wait at it during the meal, and do all the washing up, which sometimes included as many as fourteen saucepans. This uninviting work was done with sand and lemon juice, to the great detriment of her hands.

Another of Gladys's jobs was every night to carry upstairs white enamel jugs filled with hot water for the hip baths. The water would stand in the baths until the next morning, when she would empty them. Her time off was every Wednesday afternoon and every other Sunday, from 2 p.m. to 5.30 p.m. in the winter and to 7.30 p.m. in summer. Christmas was a great time in the servants' hall when all were equal and an excellent dinner provided, with presents for each member of staff, both indoor and out.

Mrs Joan Wall, who was born in Findon and lived there for most of her life, was another youngster who went straight into service as soon as she left school. She joined her sister at Muntham Court, a beautiful old mansion in Findon, now, alas, demolished. The staff consisted of butler, pantry boy, three housemaids, two parlour-maids, a cook-housekeeper and Joan herself, the fourteen-year-old kitchen-maid.

At Muntham Court the staff uniforms were somewhat unusual. The butler wore a black and orange striped waistcoat; the parlourmaids had orange cotton dresses, small black aprons with frilly edges and 'nippy' type caps with black ribbons. Joan's uniform wasn't nearly as interesting, being just a white cotton dress covered with a long white apron which, she said, was bigger than herself, for she was only a little over 4 feet tall. Whenever she scrubbed the kitchen table (which was often) she had to climb right on to it, as it was impossible for her to reach the whole surface from floor level.

Muntham Court, Findon

Joan was up in the mornings by 5.30 and her first job was to rake out the huge kitchen stove, which she referred to as the 'Monster'. She then raked the ashes to revive the fire enough to boil a kettle for a pot of tea which she took up to the cook's room.

Another young school-leaver was Mrs Florence Stringer, who eventually retired to live with and work for a friend at Ball's Cross, near Petworth. Florence started work at the age of thirteen at South Lodge, Lower Street, Beeding, earning £12 a year as scullery-maid, with all found except her uniform. This consisted of three light blue cotton frocks, six white and three coarse sacking aprons, black stockings, ward shoes and three white caps.

To purchase these her mother went with her to Horsham on what was regarded as an exciting shopping spree.

For a youngster Florence's work was very hard. She was taught how to prepare all kinds of game and she was responsible for a large number of copper pans which she cleaned with sand, vinegar and salt. Those were days before rubber gloves were available and like Gladys Baker's, her hands suffered very severely.

With part of her first earnings Florence bought herself a lipstick, which her horrified father put straight into the fire. What he didn't know was that she had bought two and the other one was safely in her bedroom.

Mrs Ada Barnet of Pulborough, who just missed celebrating her hundredth birthday in 1983, was one of the few who didn't go straight into domestic service on leaving school. Instead she went into a training school at Oakmead, near Ockley. She still remembered the seemingly endless 5 mile walk every Sunday after church, to pick up the mail.

She sat very upright in her chair as she told me some of the details of her year at Oakmead, where about twenty girls were thoroughly trained in domestic work, spending one month in each of the various branches of housework. This included scullery, parlour, laundry, cooking, sweeping and polishing as well as learning how to cope with the hated old kitchen stoves of the day. The girls ranged in age from homesick little nine-year-olds to capable and reliable young women of sixteen and seventeen.

At certain intervals during the terms there were holidays to look forward to and on these occasions Ada was always met at Ockley Station by an uncle and taken to London to stay with an aunt. This aunt practically never let her out of her sight and Ada still remembered her disappointment when she was refused permission to stay with other relations in Wales; but she was allowed to collect rents in London for her aunt and she looked forward to these spells of freedom with real pleasure.

Eventually Mrs Barnet went into service in Bury village where her salary was £25 a year, supplying her own uniform. She was very happy in the job where she got on well with the cook – an essential in the kitchen hierarchy. The cook was highly paid, receiving £56 a year. In one of her other posts where she was paid at the rate of fourpence an hour, Ada succumbed to the temptation of a superior offer of sixpence an hour from next door.

This accepted round of domestic work for the daughters of farm labourers was generally a necessity. Most of them came from large families and one less mouth to feed, plus a little extra money, was a welcome arrangement. Even if the girls were rather young to leave home and were often homesick, they had pride in their work and in their independence. This arrangement paid off well in the next generation, for the men they married were perhaps more fortunate than they may have realized in having a wife who was thoroughly trained in most branches of home-making, and this led to contented parents and happy children.

Fishermen and Boat-builders

With the Sussex coastline stretching for over 90 miles, mention must be made of the county's fishermen. Jeffery Barnes of Hunston took an almost fatherly interest in what he called 'the best winkles in the county'. He expressed a great dislike of spartini grass, for it is a mud stirrer and frequently choked some of his baby winkles. He also disliked cold weather because his winkles only flourished in clear warm waters. Jeffery was also a lobster and crab man and his family had an interesting historical connection in the annals of the fishing world. His mother was a Grant whose ancestors had the right, dating from Queen Elizabeth I, to fish the estuary for ever.

Bojam Coombes lived in Bosham all his life and joined his family in the fishing industry at the age of fourteen. They were chiefly oyster men and

Bojam Coombes

Old Bosham

Bojam was at first rated as a 'half stenceman' and was allowed to take only 300 oysters during the season. As soon as he attained the age of eighteen, he was recognized as a 'full stenceman' and thereafter permitted to take up to 600.

Another well-known fishing family was the Burtenshaws of Littlehampton. Ron made some very interesting comments on the vast changes which have taken place in the fishing industry in recent times. Talking of the old days he said, 'A fisherman's life has always been hard and still is today, in spite of everything.' Fishermen generally start out, depending on the nature of the elements, on the earliest tide, sometimes as early as 2 a.m., in order to cover the 12 miles or so to reach the fishing banks.

The herring season was an extremely busy one, lasting for only three weeks; when there was a glut the catch was sold at half-a-crown (12½p) a hundred – a fisherman's 100 being 120, just as the baker's dozen in those days was thirteen. In Ron's day, all fishermen made their own gear

Littlehampton fishermen

Bosham fishermen

Littlehampton harbour

Littlehampton fishermen

and he used to row up the Arun as far as Bury Manor to cut the osiers for his lobster pots. The fishing business was always a family concern, with grandfathers, sons and grandsons all working together.

'Today,' said Ron, 'the industry is big business with large companies supplying radar echo-sounding equipment, ship-to-shore radio, automatic navigator and pilot, power winch and even refrigerating plant. No wonder the price of fish is high. In the old days when we were unable to go out because of heavy weather, the price was never raised, however scarce the catch was.'

Some very peculiar catches have been recorded off the Sussex coast. A cod which had an unusual swelling was opened up and a sizeable pork chop was found in its stomach! On another occasion a lobster was caught which had grown an almost full-sized extra claw attached to one of its normal claws. One fisherman told me that he had found quite large stones in the stomachs of some fish – 'Quite a bonus in a fishing competition!' he said. One winter some fishing friends pulled up a plastic bag in their net and on opening it, found some false teeth.

The men who made the giant J-class yachts worked in the boatyards just over the border at Emsworth in Hampshire. Jack Dridge described the scene. 'The huge J-class yachts have gone for ever,' he said. 'Those great giants which gave employment to numbers of boat-builders and the crews to sail them will never be seen again. Their cost today would be prohibitive.' He was sad, for they were the pride and joy not only of their builders, crews and owners, but also of the countries which produced them.

At Work in the Woods

Hurdle-makers working alone in the woods see much that any casual pedestrian would certainly miss. They are aware of the slightest movements and the smallest changes that take place on their familiar ground. George Juggins, one of the old Sussex hurdle-makers, spent the whole day working in, or just outside, his little hut, often without seeing or hearing another human being. A bird or small animal would never pass unnoticed; even to see someone riding on a horse was unusual, so remote was his area.

George was very appreciative of his peaceful surroundings. 'It is a picture,' he said, as he explained the routine sequences of his lonely life, 'to see the primroses, foxgloves, bluebells and anemones which always spring up in cleared areas.'

George Juggins

Albert Searle was a hurdle-maker for sixty-six years. He said of his work: 'It isn't as easy as it looks. It all has to grow back again or you do yourself out of a job.' After some years in the noisy confusion of service abroad in the Second World War and then a short time spent gardening, he gladly returned to the hurdle-making. 'Of all those silent years spent in the woods', he said, 'I have really enjoyed the solitude.'

Another man who worked alone in the woods was Albert Peacock of Fishbourne. He learnt his craft as a spar-maker from his father, starting at the age of ten. He still demonstrates

Making a hurdle from woven cleft hazel

Albert Peacock spar making

spar-making at the Weald and Downland Open Air Museum. Albert's mother was one of those admirable women who not only bore and looked after children, at the same time running the house, doing the cooking, cleaning up and helping on the farm, but she took in washing from other people. This helped out with her husband's meagre farm wages. Mrs Peacock had five sons and five daughters all of whom had their own jobs to do, both before school and after. She did not economize on her own family washing for she took the sheets off each bed once a week, washed, dried and ironed them and returned them immediately to the beds.

When Albert was two, the family moved to Treyford Farm and from there the children walked 3 miles to the nearest school at Elsted. The schoolroom was heated by a cast-iron coke-burning stove and the smell of burning coke still reminds Mr Peacock of his schooldays. Before leaving for school each day, most of the children helped to split the spars and for this they were paid one halfpenny a day. If they had worked well they were given a mug of hot cocoa. On arrival at school, the first thing the young spar-makers had to do was to wash their hands and as there was no running water in the school they brought it with them in a bottle. Mrs Chadwick, their teacher, was strict but just and was therefore much respected. The Lord's prayer was recited at 9 a.m. and repeated at 3 p.m. before the rush for home.

As soon as the children had finished their tea, it was back to the woods to make up tidy bundles for heating the old-fashioned kitchen copper.

'When I was fourteen and a half I went into a very hard job. It was heavy, physical work in a hunting stable. I had to carry on my back sacks of wheat, lifting them off the cart and taking them up three steps to dump them in tidy two-sack-deep lines,' Mr Peacock remembered.

Thatch fixed on to a hayrick using spars

At this same early period he was breaking in young horses. Once, when he was driving a two-horse team of Shires in a field, they suddenly stopped and refused to take another step. Getting down to see what was wrong he found, lying in the long grass at the edge of the field, a sleeping child of about three years old. 'Lucky I wasn't driving a tractor,' he said as he told me the story.

As with all farm horsemen, Mr Peacock remembers with affection his Shires, Punch, Prince, Captain, Violet, Primrose, Major and Kate.

Other things made by the men in the woods were listed by 'Nobby' Kinnard. Things such as pea-sticks, bean rods and hoops for barrels: all these could be made at any time of the year. As I was leaving 'Nobby' after chatting for some time in his little hut in the woods, he said, 'Go steady! There aren't many of us left!'

Man of Many Trades

Bill Dack of Wisborough Green was a striking figure with masses of thick grey curly hair tumbling out from under his cap. He was a Sussex man with no home and was brought up, from the age of eighteen months, in a workhouse orphanage. Two things he remembered from his early days; one was that children were dosed with rhubarb medicine once a week. Of the other he said, 'I have much happier memories of Christmas morning when every child found a new penny under his plate at breakfast. We looked forward to these with tremendous excitement and I can still see the bright new coins as we lifted the plates off.'

As soon as he turned fourteen Bill joined the Royal Berks Regiment as a drummer boy. Later on he became a bugler and all his service life he was concerned with military music. 'But I haven't looked a crotchet in the face since I left the army,' he said.

When that day came he had no home to go to and no job. He found himself in Horsham and made his way on foot to Loxwood where Mr Stanbridge, of Peppers Farm, took him in. Soon he met Elsie Oakley who came daily to fetch milk and, after a five-year courtship, they married. Of these days, he said, 'I did many different jobs but I was never specifically taught anything. Among these jobs were those of a navvy, bricklayer, well-digger and sewer man. I also collected burglars,' he added, referring to a time when he became a part-time watchman.

Mr Dack was a well-known local character selling, in the village of Wisborough Green, his own home-grown vegetables from an old pram.

However, he had a self-appointed winter job making garden gnomes.

As you approached Bill's cottage you were greeted by gnomes in the window, gnomes in the grass and flowerbeds, and gnomes peeping out of the walls. There was a healthy crop waiting in a greenhouse for the summer season. 'I would never put them out in the cold,' he explained, then hastily he added, 'but I never talk to them!'

Photographers

In the 1870s there were at least two photographers in Chichester, Thomas Russell and R.N. Nally. Mrs Arnell's father, James Hart, had his photograph taken in Chichester in 1870. When asked how he would like to be done, his reply was 'Just as I be'. Mrs Arnell's mother had hers taken in her own home by R.N. Nally. She is shown sitting on a Victorian horsehair chair with an elaborate antimacassar over the back. Her dressmaker's model, made of wickerwork, stands in the background.

Engagement and Marriage

The customs regarding engagements at the turn of the century were very much stricter than they are today. The conventions were carefully observed and any girl wishing to become engaged had to bring her 'intended' home to meet the members of her own family. When she was about seventeen or eighteen Caroline Emily Lockyer was cycling on the Downs one day with a friend when they met another cyclist, an attractive young man named Will Lockyer. The three of them got along so well that for the next four years, Will cycled down from London most weekends. It was assumed that an engagement was going to take place. However, Caroline's mother wasn't going to allow her daughter to marry into a family she had not herself met and approved, so she made it her business to travel up to London to inspect Will's family before she gave her permission for the engagement to be announced. Even that wasn't enough, for Caroline herself had to be approved, and not only by Will's parents but also by his five sisters and that must have been quite an ordeal, for there was much curiosity on their part about their only brother's fiancée. All apparently went well, for the couple were married at the Worthing Tabernacle in Chapel Street when Caroline was twenty-two.

Caroline's father was one of Worthing's best-known cab proprietors and his 'fly' was the very first Worthing cab to have the new hard rubber tyres and was therefore much in demand by the local gentry.

Caring for the Children

Family illnesses could lead to quite tragic results, for if a man didn't turn up for work he wasn't paid, and the poor wives were expected to carry on feeding and clothing the family whether there was any income or not. As for the doctor, he had to be paid for at each visit. The mother of Mrs Lilian Knight of Arundel came to an arrangement with Dr Pearson by which she paid him twopence a week and when any of her children were sick the doctor always came and there were no further costs to worry about.

Mrs Vi West was one of twelve children, as also was her mother. Vi was a delicate child and had been picked out by the doctor on one of his visits to Poling village school as being in need of extra nourishment. She therefore joined the little group which every Tuesday and Thursday were given a pint of milk each, and on Mondays, Wednesdays and

The village doctor's pony and trap, used for visiting patients

Fridays received a bowl of soup. These were all supplied by Lady Johnston, wife of the African explorer Sir Harry Johnston who lived in the village. The children used to call at her home on their way to school to pick up this extra food, which they consumed during the mid-morning break under the eyes of one of Vi's brothers; this supervision wasn't at all necessary as she and the other delicate children always relished their extra rations.

Hedger and Ditcher

Some old country people find it almost impossible to give up the work that they have done for so many years. One such was Percy West who was a hedger and ditcher on the West Lavington estate. Although he was seriously disabled with arthritis in both hips, he continued and enjoyed working for many years after he had become pensionable, his sturdy spirit urging him to pursue a wide range of physical activities.

As a young man Percy had worked with cows, horses, pigs and, of course, his enormous Shire horses. He spoke lovingly of his old friends

Hedge-laying

Blossom, Prince, Captain, Violet and Kitty. In 1968 he left farming and started full time hedging and ditching. So keen was he to continue this in spite of his disability that he was presented with an invalid's blue car to carry him to and from his lanes and ditches. Talking about his work he said that he liked to think his own thoughts in peace in the shade of the trees, down in the ditches or just at the side of the road. Being on his own he saw more of nature than most people and once, when he was standing at the bottom of a fairly deeply cut ditch, a deer leapt right over him. He said he often saw foxes and vixens with their cubs whilst always remaining unseen himself. He was grateful for the little blue car and said, 'If I can keep going at my own pace I shall be quite happy.'

Percy West

Lovely to Hear and See

Besides nature, music was often appreciated and most of the old people spoke of their village concerts with warmth. They used to turn out in the winter evenings, sometimes bringing their own heating apparatus with them in the form of paraffin stoves. Lord Leconfield always supplied music for his tenants once a year on rent days when they went to Petworth House to pay their dues. Pocketing their receipts, the farmers and other tenants passed through the office into a large room where bread and cheese, cold meats and beer awaited them. Also in attendance was a local family of singers. Describing the scene Charles Wadey of Ebernoe said, 'The music was lovely to hear.' He remembered that farm workers appreciated hearing choir practice as they passed the church of an evening in their laden wagons at harvest time, keeping silent for as long as the music could be heard.

The countryman's powers of description are sometimes very vivid. 'The country was brown and purple with bracken,' was how Charles Wadey described the immediate surroundings of his cottage at Ebernoe, when recalling life there in the twenties. I thought how

The village band

Basting the horned sheep at the Ebernoe Horn Fair

unexpected it was that he should have picked out the purple which, as any painter knows, is often indistinguishable from brown in certain lights.

Describing the village of Poling as it used to be, Douglas Binsted said, 'In those days the banks were covered with primroses and violets which could be smelt long before they could be seen.' Regretting the changes which had taken place he continued, 'And we've lost many of our birds, too, including the nightingale. But I sometimes still see rabbits, squirrels and foxes, though nothing like I used to. Everyone used to help everyone else then; a cup of tea would be offered to you at any cottage at any time of the day if you had the time to spare.'

Dry Humour

Rustic wit can be very dry indeed and a countryman's sense of humour sometimes tinged with sarcasm.

Old Ernest, as he was known locally, had for many years been responsible for keeping the hedges in the area where he lived, well

Poling village. The author once lived in the flint cottage second on the left of the picture

George Weekes

trimmed and always tidy. He was really shocked when, soon after he retired (at the age of seventy-five) to a very old cottage, a dreadfully noisy and inefficient machine took his place. Threshing steel battered and tore the twigs and branches from the hedges, leaving an untidy residue of bedraggled litter in its wake. No one cleared it up – it was just left to be distributed at the will of the wind and the passing traffic.

I was driving in the district some time after Ernest's retirement, when I saw him coming my way far down the lane. I saw his bowed and gaitered legs as he came towards me. He was supported by his knobbly stick, his brown and white spaniel trotting at his heels. I drew up alongside and called out, 'Hullo, Ernest. How are you?' He gave me a sour look, waved his staff in the general direction of the sorry sight, thought for a moment and replied, 'I'm better than I would have bin if I'd bin responsible for these 'edges!'

In my own village I was talking to Charlie Hole's wife outside their cottage. Charlie worked at the local farm and was trimming the hedge with his billhook, opposite his home, taking an occasional break to converse with his fellow worker Cyril Matcham. To see us chatting was too much for him. 'You girls got nothing better to do than gossip?' he called out, poking his head over the top of the hedge.

'That's right,' replied his wife, 'and *we* aren't paid for it either!'

George Weekes of Arundel recalled an incident from the days when he was doing his war service in the motor-bike section of the RAF. One of his riders, who had already earned himself the name of Crasher Smith, came back to camp bleeding and in a state of mild shock. He explained his condition by saying he had seen two men carrying nothing. 'What do you mean, carrying nothing?' asked George. 'Well, sir,' was the reply, 'I *thought* they were carrying nothing – but it turned out to be a sheet of glass!'

Charles Mitchell, the Pyecombe crook maker

Life was Sweet

Some of these old farm workers were not averse to a bit of history, as I found when chatting one day with an old shepherd near the Saxon church at Sompting.

'That were done in the war,' said George Humphries, pointing to some ruins near by. I expressed some surprise and said that I didn't know that the Germans had bombed Sompting. He gave me a long, hard look as he replied, 'It were Cromwell and his lot!'

When he was ninety I went to see Charles Mitchell, the Pyecombe crook-maker. He was like a very lively gnome, full of fun. I was with my sister who had been drawing his portrait, which turned out to be a very good likeness, so we were both surprised when, after studying it for a while, Charles said, 'My wife won't reckernise it.' 'It's very like you,' I said, 'so why not?' ''Cos she's been dead this twenty year!' he replied, dancing up and down with delight at his little joke.

Len Ireland, head gamekeeper to Lady Herries at Arundel Park, told me that he loves every minute of his work, a great deal of which takes place at night. He uses six of the fiercest-sounding dogs I have ever heard: two alsations, which are mother and daughter; a labrador for retrieving; two spaniels for hunting and a terrier. His spaniels are clumber-cross which are considered to be steadier and heavier than pedigree spaniels. 'A gamekeeper has to be out in all weathers,' he said: 'and there are many times when we are physically uncomfortable. But the work is never boring and as a nature watch it is unrivalled.'

In 1986 the Keeper's Lodge in Arundel Park was enlarged. During the work the builders found a construction board beneath the stairs which had a very curious statement written on it in pencil. First came five signatures, followed by these words: 'DECEMBER 15th 1875. HENRY WAINWRIGHT IS TO BE HUNG NEXT TUESDAY THE 21st DECEMBER 1875 FOR THE MURDER OF HARRIET LANE. MR SHELLEY IS WITNESS TO THIS DOCUMENT.'

My curiosity was aroused, so I went to the Chichester Reference Library where I was swiftly supplied with the *West Sussex Journal* dated 30 November 1875. I was able to track down a full account of the case and I came to the conclusion that this must have been the famous Whitechapel Murder which caused nationwide interest at the time. But I was unable to find any connection with any part of Sussex.

The warm seclusion of the pubs and the social stability of life in the country in those days give a picture of basic happiness which seems to have gone for ever.

George Humphries and George Chant, both shepherds for more than sixty years

A Sussex lane, East Dean

Today, with modern social security, the old people sit back in warmth and comfort, talking of days gone by. This attitude was well described by Cyril Matcham, a one-time shepherd and horseman, who said, 'Life passes pleasantly – and sometimes too fast.'

The rough hard lives of these people seem to have left them ungrudging, though difficulties and discomforts are readily admitted. They sum up their working days in crisp, short sentences which have the ring of truth:

'The work was pretty tough but it didn't do us no harm.'

'They were happy days in spite of the difficulties.'

'My life on the farm was hard but happy.'

'I've had a rough and tough working life, but a happy one.'

'Though the work was hard and the pay low, I was happy and contented.'

The word 'happy' is constantly used when they speak of the past and this may well be due to the fact that they were satisfied to work along with their peers and their animals.

An 87-year-old woodman, Albert Roberts who, incidentally, was proud of having lived through six reigns and had spent all his life in the Sussex woodlands, summed it up in three simple words. 'Life was sweet,' he said.